the color of lost rooms

lost

rooms

Irene Latham

the color of lost rooms

Irene Latham

BLUEPRESS
ROOSTER

"What we have once enjoyed we can never lose.
All that we love deeply becomes part of us."

–Helen Keller

–for my parents

Mary Hedden Hughs and Kenneth E. Dykes Sr.,
with love and gratitude

Copyright © 2010 by Irene Latham

Blue Rooster Press
1410 Seventeenth Street South
Birmingham, Alabama 35205

Manufactured in the United States
First edition, first printing

ISBN 978-0-9762557-4-1

No part of this book may be reproduced in any form without the publisher's written consent.

Contents

i.

Why Hester Prynne Still Loves the Color Red	3
My Dress Hangs There	4
The First Time Lancelot Loved Me, This Is What He Said	5
Cherries in the Sun (Siesta)	6
Love Poem with Christmas Lights	7
Virgin of the Rocks	8
At Age Ninety My Grandfather No Longer Gardens	9
Beach Scene	10
Cowboy Song	11
Breakfast of the Birds	12
After Katrina	13
Staffelsee in Autumn	14

ii.

Black Dress	17
After One Thousand Miles the Road Rises	18

Abe Lincoln Speaks of Mary Todd	19
Black Shawl Remembers Crazy Horse	21
Einstein's Daughter Questions Her Father's Theory	22
Alligator Pears in a Basket	23
The Cage	24
Audrey Hepburn at the Dance Studio	25
The Institut de Beauté on Marszalkowska Street	26
Lady Clementine Churchill at the Semiramis Hotel	27
When the Day Comes	28
Abandoned Cottage (County Galway)	29
Still Life with Watermelon, Pears and Grapes	31

iii.

Blue Still Life	35
Postcard from Mars	36
Jacqueline Picasso Ends Her Life	37
Anne Moynet Audubon, Long before *Birds of America*	38
Pontoon Boat in May	39

Ida Straus, after *The Titantic*	41
Baby Ruth's Letter to Dolly Dimple, 1941	43
Living Room	44
Plate 13 from *Dissertation in Insect Generations and Metamorphosis*	45

iv.

Oyster	49
Sheep by the Sea	51
Back to the Hills of Georgia	52
The Bath	53
In My Mother's Dream	54
Irene Curie Teaches Her Sister to Ride a Bike	55
Flying Lessons	56
Simplicity 8953	58
How the Sacagawea River Got Its Name	59
The Faith of Spiders	60
The Shepherd David	61
Keepsake	63
CREDITS	65
ACKNOWLEDGMENTS	67

i.

Why Hester Prynne Still Loves the Color Red

Because my whole body became
an ocean of red-tipped waves
        brutal
                relentless

and it brought me a baby
with skin so white I could only
        think
                Pearl.

Shall we lay out our lives,
my jagged edge to your
        crooked
                line?
I recognize that flush, the way
your hand keeps climbing
        your
                neck.

What tenderness there is in drowning.

My Dress Hangs There

–after the painting by Frida Kahlo

When the maid asks, *must you leave*
New York so soon? I will say, *it is*
just the smell of last week's uneaten fruit

that makes me long for La Casa Azul.
Then I will fold my lies into a suitcase,
and carry my pain to Mexico

where it can live a colorful life
under skirts that swirl as I raise
the brush, paint myself again and again,

until finally I see glimpses not of me
but of who I will become. I could say
I will miss you, but I won't

and when my back aches, I will paint
and when I am hungry, I will paint
and when I want to be loved
I will rest beneath the mango tree.

The First Time Lancelot Loved Me, This Is What He Said

Let me look at you

so I lifted my arms,
unpinned my hair

That bright moon in its fullness?
It speaks of love that cannot be

allowed the gown to singe
each strawberry nipple
as it drifted down
down

There is a reason kingdoms have fallen

Cherries in the Sun (Siesta)

–after the painting by Doris Lee

You can sleep when you're dead,
Mama said. I never once saw

her unstrap her shoes, walk
barefoot through fresh-cut

grass. When the rooster
crowed, she leapt out of bed

and did not return for many
hours. Mama, I don't believe

in roosters. I believe in cherries,
ripe and throbbing, every afternoon.

Love Poem with Christmas Lights

That first Christmas without
your mother, I watched you unpack

a box marked *Decorations*. First
you unfurled the crumpled garland,

straightened the plaid ribbon
and worked to reshape the swag

into something resembling evergreen.
Then you set about repairing

the broken hooks on plastic ornaments,
broken plastic attached to intact hooks.

And when the string of lights failed
to blink, even after you removed

the busted bulbs and twisted
new ones in their place, you shook

your head and said, *I can't fix this.*
Then you gently placed the lights

back inside the box, gathered wrench
and ratchet, began to build our son a bike.

Virgin of the Rocks

–after the painting by Leonardo da Vinci

He knows metal-point
cannot capture her skin,
nor red chalk; only

thick, tinted oil.
He releases the buckle,
the endless plait

of hair, gathers
her like water
through a tangled

net. She watches him
fill the jug with tender
precision, learns

love is delicate
as a knot on a scabbard,
gold- tooled and interwoven.

At Age Ninety My Grandfather No Longer Gardens

No time, he says, as he lifts my grandmother
from her wheelchair to the toilet and back again

spoons rice and cubed JELL-O past unsmiling lips
into her gaping baby-bird mouth

then eases her onto the sofa, careful
to tuck the beaded flannel beneath her chin.

Meanwhile, what was once jubilant rows
of tassled corn and sturdy pole beans

now snarls like a half-starved dog
whose coat is thick with burrs and tangles,

and as my grandmother's breath shuffles in and out
my grandfather dreams of tomatoes:

fat Beefsteak and juicy Better Boys,
Early Girls blushing pink then flaming red,

remembers summers spent weeding and watering,
how he'd palm the tomatoes, give them the slightest twist,

then sit back on his heels as the fruit burst
like fireworks against the back of his teeth.

Beach Scene

–after the painting by Jane Peterson

Sand in drifts,
parade of skin:
peach, pink,

ruddy, lobster.
Heat prickles,
tempers flare

bare feet sink,
splash, dash
buckets, shovels

tossed aside
for waves,
sea salt, foam.

Ocean grumbles,
roars, later
whispers,

I'm sorry
shhhhh
yes.

Cowboy Song

go tend
the barbed wire

while I wait
on the shuck
mattress

red roof unhinged
and ripening

Breakfast of the Birds

–after the painting by Gabriele Minter

Curtain opens,
day after Christmas:

birds perch
like ornaments

on snowy branches,
feast on given

seed. She holds
her applause,

recalls yesterday's
fury of paper

and ribbon,
all the scripted

squabbles.
Would take her

leave, if not for
this intermission.

After Katrina

She loosens laces, widens mouth
of soggy shoes, then leaves them
to dry on the weathered railing where
they soon sprout pine straw

and a wren darts out—four pink
eggs hidden just beneath the tongue.
She backs into the house, careful
not to let the screen door slap shut,

and for a heartbeat she is neither
grateful nor resentful, just a woman
pressing her toes into warm linoleum,
pulling apart a piece of day-old bread.

Staffelsee in Autumn

–after the painting by Gabriele Munter

When the trees kindle
their fires, when the sky

dissolves the lake and all
the small mysteries

are magnified: the scar
on your elbow, freckled

left earlobe, each line
and hollow accounted for

and made sacred.
We cannot hold onto

these days. A sharp wind
cuts the water into sheets

of ice, leaves crinkle
and curl, the easy gifts

of acorn and walnut
are buried, devoured.

Our fingerprints no
longer visible as breath.

ii.

Black Dress

–for my mother

Handmade with love
the label declared,

and still I placed
the dress in a garbage

bag, left it at the curb
for a truck to carry away.

Now your joints swell,
your sewing machine

stays covered, and I
have money for dresses.

But I want them back,
those dresses I watched

you cut from satin sheets—
the black dress, out of style

now, but classic the way
black dresses are,

how we learn about love
too late.

After One Thousand Miles the Road Rises

Pheasant season, he says, then points
to wide Dakota prairies broken by dark dots
of distant cows and bison grazing wheat,

and I am his girl again as truck roars
past fields of blackened sunflowers and wells
pulling smooth oil, past rusting carcasses

of machinery parked on high hilltops,
past buttes and snow fences and towns
with names like Medora and Mandan

and Sturgis. My father drives us into
moonless night, says to me, *the strength
of a tree comes not from growing thicker*

*in the good wet years, but from surviving
the endless dry times,* and as his face
disappears in shadow and reappears

in oncoming headlights, I know the dry
times are coming and the harvest won't wait.

Abe Lincoln Speaks of Mary Todd

She's bold as a blackberry, my Molly
and it's true, I love her

but a man who grows up in the woods
knows a trap when he sees one,

a man who's spent whole days
chopping lumber knows pine splits

different from oak and you can't
approach one the way you would the other.

A man who's lived off the land
knows the cunning of fox,

the resourcefulness of bear.
As soon as she turned those tart

blue eyes from mine, I knew
the baby was a lie.

and that's why tomorrow
I'm going to marry her.

She doesn't know it, but I can
read her like I can name the track

of every beast native to Indiana.
I know where she's been

and where she wants to take me.
A man who grows up in the woods

knows the wild will always be wild,
and love is not about taming.

Black Shawl Remembers Crazy Horse

The old ones like to say
memory is like riding a trail
at night with a lighted torch.
And so it does not surprise me
that your face has been swallowed
by darkness, your voice black as
the wounded wings of a crow.

But sometimes the torch flares,
illuminating the way your body
folded itself against mine,
how the last time you loved me
you dipped your thumb in red paint
and covered the part in my hair,
marking me a woman greatly loved.

When the rattlesnake came into
the lodge, you could not crush it.
And you couldn't save our daughter
from the white man's coughing disease.
In the end, the Black Hills were lost, too—
the heart of everything that is.

I wasn't your only wife. But I am
the one who remembers.

Einstein's Daughter Questions Her Father's Theory

It's all about timing, he says.
She watches the circling second-hand
as it marks all the moments he's missed,

says, *space-time is a lump of clay
whose geometry can be changed
by the gravity of stars and planets.*

And I am neither clay nor star nor planet.

It was best for you, he says.
Her jaw tightens, fists clench.
I am not a spinning orb, she says.

*Must you strap the fabric
of the universe to my back,
demand that I drag it behind me?*

It must be proven, he says.

She shakes her head. *It's as real
as a wobbling spiral of gas
that disappears into a black hole.*

It changes nothing, he says. And she
climbs back inside her super-
luminal tunnel, leave him to his work.

Alligator Pears in a Basket

–after the painting by Georgia O'Keefe

Eat, his mother said. *You must
clean your plate.* He crossed
his arms and clamped his teeth.
Sat at the table for hours.

By bedtime his mother's eyes
blazed. *You can't make me,*
the boy said, and the pears
came alive, their jaws snapping,
their leathery skin slapping
against his tender cheek.

And then they all went to bed:
the pears, the plate, the mother
and finally, the boy. His eyes
half-closed, ever watchful.

The Cage

–after the painting by Berthe Morisot

Banished to a world
without rain

they huddle inside
the gilded wire,

wings battened
against the memory

of storm:
feathers, screech,

the bag that blinds.
So soft, the hands

that betray.
Thunderbolt eyes,

cloud-cracking
light.

The only song—
such a pretty pair

Audrey Hepburn at the Dance Studio

Born for arabesque and cabriole,
I could not pirouette my way

through the occupation, could only
perform in my mind pique turns

and side leaps while I scratched
dirt with fingers, unearthed

tulip bulbs and ground them
to flour. Between loaves

my bones began to wither
and crack, hunger dissolving

the fine arches of my feet,
the graceful curve of calf.

When the war ended I stumbled
into a different dream.

And for all it's given me
and all I've become, I'd trade it

for this mirror, this bar,
one night on some great stage,

my body fluid as sunlight
breaking over a field of wheat.

The Institut de Beauté on Marszalkowska Street

–Warsaw, Poland, 1943

We are no different, Mrs. Walter
says to Mrs. Rozenblum's back
as she uses a cotton ball to paint
the dull black locks with bleach.

Then she sweeps the hair away
from Mrs. Rozenblum's forehead,
pulls the hairbrush hard against
the scalp to banish any kinks.

Wear grey, she says. *Put away
the eyeglasses, the scarf.
Learn the Lord's Prayer and
wear a cross.* Mrs. Rozenblum

squeezes her eyes the way she does
when the butcher lifts his knife.
Remember, Mrs. Walter says.
If the police stop you, look them

in the eye. Then she slams down
the hairbrush, grabs her customer's
cheeks until her eyes pop open. *Look
them in the eye, or you will disappear.*

Lady Clementine Churchill at the Semiramis Hotel

–Cairo, 1921

I hate camels, she said after
the day-long ride to the Sphinx.
She sank lower into the copper tub,

tried to forget about her aching thighs
as she scrubbed away the colorless
desert and breathed deep the fragrance

of clover blowing in from the far
riverbank. Where did Winston put
his paint box, the tubes of ochre

and vermilion, brush caked with oil
and begging to be cleaned? *A map
would be more useful*, she thought

as she examined the sand-streaked
canvas with its slanting palm trees,
black against the tangerine sky.

When the Day Comes

–in memory of Maggie Evelyn Dennis Dykes

Walk the path to the ocean,
lift a smooth stone and bend
to examine the shape
left in sand, watch it fill

with water. Climb the dunes,
find an open caterpillar
casing, a just-born butterfly
fluttering its wings

in this overwhelming world
of light. Then, a spider's web—
sticky, empty threads a miracle
not to the spider, but to those

who grieve. As you gather
sea glass and shards of shell,
listen for that grace-filled
moment after the last bird call

but before the crickets.
Follow the sun's slow slide,
how it leaves behind pink
streaked clouds.

Abandoned Cottage (County Galway)

–after the painting by Virginia Berresford

And this is where
we shall meet:
in the shuttered house

built by shepherds
who grew weary
of rain-swept nights

and wakefulness,
their backs pressed
against rocky soil.

So they stacked stone,
thatched a roof.
Inside, a small fire

kept them warm
and blankets softened
their sleep. On clear

nights the shepherds
dreamed dreams
without wolves.

Let us remember
them when the wolves
come: the shepherds,
the sheep, the sturdy walls.

Still Life with Watermelon, Pears and Grapes

–after the painting by Lilly Martin Spencer

And for a time
we lived our lives as gods:

when we were hungry,
we found feast.

We devoured the world,
we challenged all limits.

We took joy in naming
and claiming,

we marveled
over odd shape and contour,

the unexpected prickle
on tongue.

We celebrated *all* bodies,
not just our own,

exclaimed over the raw strength
clothed in such tender skin.

We believed the sweetness
would sustain us,

so we set our hearts
on the stone slab.

There we discovered bitter
seed, tough rind.

We were not brave enough
to call it *regret*

until many years later.

iii.

Blue Still Life

–after the painting by Anne Shreve

Past the half-opened
door that allows a view

of the garden, beyond
the vase filled with pink

sprigs and fresh water,
a cluttered table.

Imagine how the cup
misses the weight of tea,

how lonely the latch
when the door is ajar,

how the breeze keens
against the glass.

Soon the flowers will
drop their blossoms,

someone will clear away
the breakfast dishes,

the floorboards will wrawl
as the day disappears.

Postcard from Mars

Landed on Endurance Crater last night. The dunes
bristle, rake the bones of constellations riddled by
shriveled buttercups. You would have loved our hike
across Columbia Hills. Buckling floors, plucky sand.
Mother got space sick, but the rest of us kept going
until we got to Keystone. Beware the pitchpipe hum.
I could say the crags and craters shine like pie crust
brushed with egg wash. I could say I snapped on my
slicker, that we found blueberries at Eagle Crater.
But I refuse to warble that firefangled song. Instead,
I'll plait ribbons, paint a picket fence. In the roost,
nothing but bricks and bread. Would you have
chosen me if I could have given you trees? At least
the weather's been nice. Hasn't rained a drop.

Jacqueline Picasso Ends Her Life

Without him
her skin fell
into blue lines

her eyes
were shattered
by ghosts,

neck and arms
plundered by
those innocent

of the simple
faith of women
who choose

to love
the unfaithful.
He was good

to me, she thought,
just before she
pulled

the trigger.
He painted
me with flowers.

Anne Moynet Audubon, Long before *Birds of America*

This boy would dart off before dawn,
climb trees, examine eggs, take out
his little pencil and draw the birds in flight.

When I'd meet him at the arbor with tea
and cookies, he'd share the bounty
of pockets: egg shells, nests of curling

leaves, feathers of every color. So what
if his cheeks stayed smudged and he rarely
made it in time for supper? For those

of you who'll say, *he was not yours*,
I ask you: Does the earth not belong
to the sky? Does the shore not love

the ocean, even as it crashes upon it?
Does the bluebird not sit on the nest,
even if the egg is speckled instead of pale?

Pontoon Boat in May

Fishermen cast their silky lines,
careful to dodge logs submerged

just below the surface, fill the slack
moments with tales of last year's

ice storm and the curious work
of beavers. We learn the lake is fed

by three creeks: Pruitt Fork,
Claylick and Buffalo Branch.

We learn there would be no lake
if not for the dam. And I close

my eyes, see the water pouring
across the threshold, drawing

hot sparks from the outlets
as it climbs the wall. My dress

puffs around my waist like a lost
cloud as I search the rising tide

for the picture from my parents'
first wedding, when she glowed

and he believed a baby would
change everything. I see the frame

float past, photograph faded,
glass gone. Motor whirrs, sun pulls

at my cheeks. Steady stream hollows
the places hardened by blame.

Ida Straus, after *The Titantic*

If you decided to visit,
take Isidor's leather
satchel as your souvenir,

or my pearl-handled
hairbrush, now bald
of bristles. I offer you

an unopened bottle
of French perfume,
even the ruby brooch

Isidor pinned to my gown
the night we celebrated
forty years of marriage.

But I beg you: please
don't take my shoes.
I've left them lodged

in the silt beside the hull,
where I pretend
it's a dressing room,

my shoes waiting
for me to step into
them and shimmer

across a parquet floor,
Isidor's hand
at the small of my back.

Baby Ruth's Letter to Dolly Dimple, 1941

You'll be happy to know I've gained back those 200 pounds
I lost to pneumonia. Which means that for once, the Ringling
Brothers poster is true: *815 pounds*. Old Willoughby still
comes by from time to time with his measuring tapes.

He always asks about you. Remember that awful knot
on my knee? Doctor said it had to come off. So they took me
to the surgery room where five nurses hoisted me onto a table.
Then there was a crackling sound, and next thing I knew

I was on the floor! Me and Joe laughed so hard the walls
started to shake. Doctor said he'd have to order a special
operating table, just for me. I flashed him my best smile
and said, *better make it quick*. The pain's not that bad.

But when I stand in front of my three-way mirror, that knot
makes me feel ugly. And I've never felt that way before.
Not once. What'll I do if it starts affecting my appetite?
Come visit, Dolly. We'll stay up all night and eat spaghetti pie.

Living Room

There is no mystery
anymore, not in this room
or elsewhere, no phone call

answered before the caller
is identified, no baby born
whose wholeness

has not yet been established.
Even the leather chair
strips to foam and cotton

stuffing, begs to be hoisted,
thrown, torn from the room
it has not so much shared

as been parked in all these
years. I should have
asked more of you.

And you should have paid
more attention, made
the small repairs love requires.

Plate 13 from *Dissertation in Insect Generations and Metamorphosis*

–after the hand-colored engraving by Maria Sibylla Merian

By the time the casing
falls away, they no longer

recognize themselves.
They reach for each other

but it is too soon.
They must wait

for the wings to dry.
Finally, a flutter.

Slowly, so slowly
they become supple

and begin to uncurl.
Sometimes they startle

each other. One will dip,
turn, float with the current.

And the other will fly
in a different direction.

iv.

Oyster

On the beach
every living thing
yearning:

birds, apples,
the yammering wasp.
Pearls sing, quiet

chaos. Rooted
no more,
he arches open.

Listen to the wild
sway. It's hard
to carry the mouth,

the teeth, the dark
walls of fire.
So she scatters

herself like clouds
of sweet rain
from a great

distance. How
happy the world
when voices

echo moth wings.
Before they learn
the color

of lost rooms.
Look, he says.
And the streetlights weep.

Sheep by the Sea

–after the painting by Rosa Bonheur

Take away the gulls,
the scampering crabs,
the surge of waves

on a wind-carved shore.
Make it overcast, grey,
the sand full of burrs.

Think of sour milk
in a breakfast bowl,
a stagnant, brimming

barrel. Put in cliffs,
draw in some sheep
with their legs folded,

their wooly heads turned
by unyielding rock
and the loyalty of grass.

Back to the Hills of Georgia

to the white double-wide
where my brothers splashed
in the cracked plastic pool,
their laughter ripe and clear-seeded

to those abundant mornings
that smelled of peach blossoms
and baby powder where I watched
from my mother's lap, my dimpled

thighs white like hers,
my life already mapped out:
Cloudland Canyon, Mt. Cheaha,
Rock City, Mammoth Cave

to the Atlantic Ocean with its
grey beaches and wind-whipped oaks
and I want to pick that baby girl up
place her in the pool, say *look,*

the sooner you learn to swim the better.

The Bath

–after the etching by Mary Cassatt

As water sings
its abiding hymn

she blesses each
supple fold

hands never
more reverent

even as her mind
turns to Ivory

and talcum,
cotton swabs

and lightly
scented oil.

*Hush little baby,
the cradle*

will not fall.
She learns duty—

another name
for love.

In My Mother's Dream

We were silver cups
and we glistened
the way babies do
when they are still
supple as raindrops,
before the sharp

angle of elbow
and knee crowd
the birth canal
and age begins
to reveal the tiny
dents and tarnishes.

In the dream we
were unbreakable
and my mother
was whole. We
were not contained
by hook or shelf,

we fell into the right
hands. We were
silver cups, and she
drank from us, one
by one, until she was
full, and we were gone.

Irene Curie Teaches Her Sister to Ride a Bike

Like this, she says and pumps
the pedals. Eve settles in,
her narrow ankles lifting

the small feet that turn
the pedals that turn the wheels
that move the bike away.

Irene rushes to keep up, hand
hovering in the air above the seat,
anticipating the sudden waver,

the inevitable loss of balance.
She wonders if this is what it's like
to be radium, hidden by lead.

She wonders if this is what it's like
to be an atom: splitting and splitting
and splitting again.

Flying Lessons

To lift
like they do,
fugitive

white flashes
erupting

from the tribal
chamber
of pines

to seize
a sweetgrass

field where
beehives
simmer,

their vigilant
music

compensation
for the stubborn-
ness of time

and disobedience
of walls,
the wind

itself
is revolution.

Simplicity 8953

The pattern promises to make a princess
so I gather tulle, organza, duchess satin and dupioni silk

to spin a girl's dream: flouncy slip beneath shimmering skirt,
puffy sleeves, bodice edged with beaded rosette trim.

Just before dawn I add a tuck and hand-stitch the hem.
Later, as she prances and twirls, I pack away

the scissors but keep thread in my needle
should white steeds dissolve into skittering mice,

the royal coach to a pumpkin, the prince caught
dancing with someone else.

How the Sacagawea River Got Its Name

Lewis and Clark said *Sacagawea*
was for the way she carried herself,
body like a cottonwood in the wind,

silken hair rushing like late snowmelt.
She mothered and nursed, guided
them as if they were cubs, at once

protective and resigned. They wanted
to give her more than the ocean,
something bigger than the whale

carcass they watched her climb into,
something more lasting than the spears
she carved for them out of bone.

They were grateful for her patience
with words like *aster, anemone, bell.*
She shared their need to name things

and never mocked their maps, even
though she was certain paper could
not contain river, prairie, nor stand of pine.

The Faith of Spiders

so many hours
        in the shadowed corner—

not a single twitch in all those legs

not a grumble
        not a curse

about the distance between branches
or the afternoon lost to rain—

        and when the fly fumbles

or the wind
        rips a seam

or the dog in its eagerness
plunders the silver center—

the spider simply
        spins
                again

The Shepherd David

–after the painting by Elizabeth Jane Gardner

What he thinks
he wants

is to hold a woman
the way he holds

the lamb. But
tenderness

will not sustain
him. See the arm

raised in victory?
He may not

yet understand
the hunt,

but he is already
an expert

on hunger.
Soon

he will bore
of docility.

He will cast aside
the lamb,

seek the company
of lions.

Keepsake

A photograph of us
not together
but on the same beach,
a sandswept bungalow

with shoes beside the door.
Nothing in it was ours,
and when the sun set,
everything disappeared,

even *we* disappeared,
those selves made
of shell, the translucent
walls heavy with the scent

of sea. How time
softens when we share
space, how motion escapes
metaphor and defies

the definition a shore
might provide,
or the curve of a wave—
and we emerge

as crash and croon,
the whole world
reclaimed in a slip
of light beneath the door.

CREDITS

Thank you to the editors of the following publications in which some of these poems first appeared, sometimes in slightly different form:

Birmingham Weekly: "Jacqueline Picasso Ends Her Life"

Breakwater Review: "Alligator Pears in Basket" and "Still Life with Watermelon, Pears and Grapes"

Einstein at the Odeon Café: "Abe Lincoln Speaks of Mary Todd" and "Black Shawl Remembers Crazy Horse"

Free Lunch: "Einstein's Daughter Questions Her Father's Theory" and "My Dress Hangs There"

Limestone Dust Poetry Anthology: "Ida Strauss, After the Titanic," "The First Time Lancelot Loved Me, This is What He Said" and "Audrey Hepburn at the Dance Studio"

Motif 1—Writing by Ear: "Cowboy Song" as "After Listening to Norah Jones"

Motif 2—Come What May: "After Katrina"

PMS poemmemoirstory: "The Institute de Beaute on Marszalkowska Street"

POEM: "How the Sacagawea River Got Its Name"

Poems from the Big Table: "Black Dress"

Red Mountain Review: "Keepsake" as "Just Ours"

ACKNOWLEDGMENTS

Thanks, as ever, to the Big Table Poets, for your helpful comments along the way. To Jerri Beck, Peter Huggins, Bonnie Roberts, Marianne Worthington and all the poets at Colrain Poetry Manuscript Conference (August, 2010): your editing skills made a tremendous difference in this manuscript. I am forever grateful.

To Jim Reed and Russell Helms, thanks for your support of this project. Unending thanks to the women in my life, who see me through the lost rooms: Isobel Abel, Sally Allen, Lynn Baker, Vonda Braswell, Susan Brunner, Carol Burnett, Lori Ditoro, Jennifer L. Dykes, Jennifer M. Dykes, Martha Elkins, Rhonda Gregg, Mary (Mama) Hughs, Jana Hutcheson, Phyllis Larsh, Lindsey Leavitt, Trina Lester, Julie Miles, Liz Reed, Sheila Renfro, Kirie Reveron, Lisa Rogers, Randee Sims, Pam Toler, Pat Weaver, Jan Young and so many others. I'm sorry there's not space to name you all.

Special thanks to Papa (Kenneth E. Dykes Sr.), who shares my love of poetry and was able to keep me motivated and inspired over the course of several years. Papa, your many notes with names to research

are precious to me still. And to the National Museum of
Women in the Arts, thanks for the inspiration I found
in your stunning collection. Finally, to Paul, Daniel,
Andrew, Eric: thanks for sharing these rooms for so many
years. I love you.

also by Irene Latham

Leaving Gee's Bend

What Came Before

visit her at www.irenelatham.com